EVERY D

with Je

FOR GROWING CHRISTIANS

GW00786594

SHARING YOUR
FAITH

BY SELWYN HUGHES

QUIET TIME

Who can see
what goes on behind
walls of houses and
walls of faces?
Do bright lights
camouflage conflict
and brokenness?
Do bright smiles
hide heartache
and emptiness?
You can see, God
YOU know.

As I grow to know You
more clearly,
let ME see through
those walls
of bright lights
and bright smiles
to the conflict and
heartache.
Let ME carry Your
light of love
and healing
into the darkness
behind the walls.

Susan Lenzkes
© by author

LIFT JESUS HIGHER

For Reading and Meditation: John 12:23–36

" 'But I, when I am lifted up from the earth, will draw all men to myself.' " (v. 32)

The world is waiting for good news. Anxiously men and women scan the headlines of the morning papers, searching for some glimmer of light in the slow dark development of international politics. To say that the people of this age are unhappy is to say the least. They are sick. For too long humanity has been fed upon a diet of extreme optimism and despairing pessimism. There is a need for a change.

Where then can we turn for a glimmer of hope in the present world situation? Is it to the scientist, the philosopher or the politician? No. World leaders have had their chance. The only hope for this planet is to hear, from the lips of those who have experienced Christ's transforming power, the good news of the Gospel.

THE HIGHEST PRIORITY

Next to worship, the bold proclamation of our faith is, therefore, the highest priority of the Christian Church, and we must commit ourselves to this task with boldness and enthusiasm. The closing years of this century can and may well be the most powerful, penetrating and rewarding period for the spreading of the Gospel since the Church began. Christ's Gospel is only effective as it is proclaimed. It must not be apologised for, watered down, or adjusted to suit the interests of this modern age – nor should it be disguised so that it gets past an unbeliever's guard. On this first day of our readings together, let us dedicate ourselves to the task of lifting Jesus higher and, by every means available, spreading abroad His fame. In the language of our own day, we must say with Charles Wesley, "O let me commend my Saviour to you".

Christ's Gospel is only effective as it is proclaimed.

O Father, help me, during these first few days, to have a new encounter with You and with Your Son. And then help me to do something about sharing it. In Jesus' Name. Amen.

THE GREAT COMMISSION
For Reading and Meditation: Mark 16:15–20

"... 'Go into all the world and preach the good news to all creation.' " (v. 15)

W e began yesterday by affirming that, next to worship, the highest priority of the Christian Church is the bold proclamation of our faith.

Let us make one thing quite clear before going any further – the urgency of evangelism does not arise from the call of Christian leaders, for they only repeat and re-echo what Christ first said. The words, "Go ye", are chiselled into the bedrock of the Christian Church by its Master Builder and, no matter what happens, they can never be obliterated or removed. If words mean anything, then it is quite clear from what Jesus is saying in this passage that He intended the *Great Commission* to take precedence over every other form of church activity.

"GO YE INTO ALL THE WORLD ..."
When a proposal to evangelise the heathen was brought before the Scottish Church in 1796, it was met by a resolution that "to spread the Gospel to the heathen nations is highly preposterous – philosophy and learning must, in the nature of things, take precedence." Upon hearing this, Thomas Erskine called out to the Moderator, "Pass me that Bible." Turning to the sixteenth chapter of Mark's Gospel, he read to the whole assembly the words: "Go ye into all the world, and preach the gospel." Observers said that, such was the force and power of Erskine's reading, the words of the Great Commission burst over their heads like a clap of thunder. I hope, with all my heart, that these words will burst with the same explosive force in every section of Christ's Church this very day.

Jesus intended the Great Commission to take precedence over every other form of church activity.

O God, having put my hand to the plough I do not intend to look back. This shall be no halfway business. You command and I obey. Show me how to share my faith with ever-increasing effectiveness. In Jesus' Name. Amen.

AN ANGEL AT ITS HEART

For Reading and Meditation: Matthew 28:1–8

"The angel said to the women, 'Do not be afraid ...
He is not here; he has risen ...' " (vv. 5–6)

Having considered the importance and urgency of evangelism, it is time now to ask ourselves: What do we
mean by "evangelism"?

THE PROCLAMATION OF GOOD NEWS

The word "evangelism" was in use long before New Testament times, and was used mainly to describe some welcome
announcement from the Emperor proclaimed in the Greek-
speaking provinces of the Roman world. Evangelism is,
therefore, the proclamation of good news.

PLAYING THE ANGEL

There is a charming story told of the famous painter and
sculptor, Michelangelo, which tells how once, while visiting
a friend, he pointed to a huge block of marble and said, "An
angel is imprisoned in that stone and I am going to let him
out." The word "evangelism" is rather like that block of
marble. There is an angel at its heart. Subtract the first and
last syllables and what do you have left? "Angel". To evangelise is quite literally to "play the angel". The announcement of the good news that Christ was born in Bethlehem,
given by the angels in Luke 2:10, was true evangelism.

The best modern definition of evangelism is no doubt
that of the *Lausanne Covenant,* drawn up in 1974, which
says, "Evangelism is the proclamation of the historical,
Biblical Christ as Saviour and Lord, with a view to per-
suading people to come to Him personally and so be rec-
onciled to God." Although the word "evangelism" is used
in Christian circles to describe almost any endeavour of the
Christian Church, I shall limit the word in these studies to
the proclamation of the good news of God in Jesus Christ
to those who do not know Him.

*Evangelism
is the
proclama-
tion of the
good news of
God in Jesus
Christ to
those who
do not know
Him.*

Loving, heavenly Father, how can I be silent about You? If I
were, the very stones would cry out. Save me from silence
when so much is at stake. In Jesus' Name. Amen.

THE STARTING POINT

For Reading and Meditation: Matthew 28:9–20

*"Then Jesus came to them and said, 'All authority
in heaven and on earth has been given to me.
Therefore go and make disciples ...' " (vv. 18–19)*

A lthough most Christians would agree that evangelism
means the sharing of the good news of God in Jesus
Christ, there is not the same agreement on the way in
which that Good News should be spread.

And let's face it, there is room for a wide difference of
opinion here. Some believe the best way of witnessing to an
unbelieving world is to put on large evangelistic rallies in
football stadiums. Others believe the best way is by individual witness. Still others believe all evangelism ought to
be channelled through the local church. One minister I
know says – and he has a point: "Para-church organisations
are not God's way of winning people to Himself. We must
move as one body of people (the local church) into our
local area, and this means no one must go off on their own
and do their own thing evangelistically."

We all have different views and opinions on how best to
go about the work of evangelism and, as I have said, there is
room in the Christian Church for these differences.

STARTING AND FINISHING POINTS

*The early
Christians
began by
affirming
clearly and
categorically
that Jesus is
Lord.*

Having said that, however, there are two things on which
there can be no difference of opinion if our evangelism is
to be considered as Biblical evangelism. They are a kind of
starting point and *finishing point* – two issues about which
no division can be tolerated. And what are they? Jesus
announces them in the passage before us today. He
says: (1) "All authority has been given to me" and (2) "Go
and make disciples." Our starting point is, therefore, quite
clear. We begin our evangelism at the same point the early
Christians began it, by affirming clearly and categorically
that Jesus is Lord.

**Lord Jesus, help me to begin where the Gospel begins – with
submission to Your authority as Lord. Show me that unless I
crown You Lord of all, I do not crown You Lord at all. Amen.**

IS JESUS LORD?

For Reading and Meditation: I Corinthians 12:1–3

"... no-one can say, 'Jesus is Lord,' except by the Holy Spirit." (v. 3)

W e said yesterday that while there is room in the Church for differences of opinion on the methods by which the good news of God in Jesus Christ is made known, no differences can be tolerated regarding the starting point and finishing point – namely the authority of Christ and the making of disciples.

Evangelism *begins* in submission to the fact that Jesus Christ is Lord. Why is this so necessary? What does the authority of Jesus have to do with sharing our faith? It means, firstly, that we do not see *ourselves* as saviours. The temptation we fall into when we begin to share Christ is to draw attention to ourselves and thus become reformers rather than evangelists. Submission to Christ's authority means that we see ourselves as servants and not masters. We are not better than others – although, of course, better off. We are not cleverer than others. We are not superior to others.

PEDLARS OF GOD'S WORD

Paul said, in writing to the Corinthians, "For we are not, like so many, pedlars of God's word; but as men of sincerity, as commissioned by God, in the sight of God we speak in Christ" (2 Corinthians 2:17, RSV). The phrase "pedlars of God's word" is arresting. Pedlars peddle their wares for their own ends. How many Christians peddle God's Word to gain attention, to put themselves in the limelight or to satisfy their ego? There is just enough truth in this to make it sting.

We cannot go any further until each one of us personally settles this issue. How can I ask other people to make Jesus the centre of their lives if He is not the centre of mine? I must ask myself: Who is in charge of my life – me or Christ?

Evangelism begins in submission to the fact that Jesus Christ is Lord.

O God, save me from becoming a pedlar of Your Word – someone using Your Gospel for self-centred ends. Make me instead a proclaimer of it – someone who, in proclaiming the Perfect, becomes more perfect. Amen.

THE ULTIMATE GOAL

For Reading and Meditation: John 15:1–11

" 'This is to my Father's glory, that you bear much fruit, showing yourselves to be my disciples.' " (v. 8)

Having examined the starting point of all evangelism – the authority of Christ – we move on now to consider its goal, or finishing point: turning converts into disciples.

CONVERTS INTO DISCIPLES

The ultimate aim of all Biblical evangelism is to "make disciples". Jesus Christ has not called us primarily to put up buildings, publish magazines or organise special Christian events. These things may well be necessary, but they are not our *primary* task. The specific command Christ gives us here means that we are not to be content with simply seeing people come to Christ, but we are to follow their progress with the utmost care and concern until their lives reflect the glory of God and the character of Jesus Christ.

SHARING THEIR FAITH

Several years ago a dear friend of ours brought a young married couple, living in the wealthy "stockbrokers' belt" in Virginia Water, Surrey, to Christ. Not satisfied with simply leading them to Christ, she followed their progress with deep, prayerful concern. When, after a little while, they moved to the United States, she emphasised to them the need of finding a "live" Christian church and of going on with Christ. Daily she prayed for them until news came that they had found a church and were growing by leaps and bounds in the things of God. Not so long ago I spent a little time in their beautiful home near Washington D.C., and I could not help but marvel at the way they had grown in Christ and were now reaching out to share their faith with others. They were now more than just "converts" – they were well and truly "disciples". Evangelism is not complete until the evangelised become evangelists.

Evangelism is not complete until the evangelised become evangelists.

Gracious heavenly Father, thank You for showing me that the purpose of all evangelism is that the evangelised become evangelists. Help me not only to save a soul but to make a disciple. In Jesus' Name. Amen.

THE SUSTAINING ASSURANCE

For Reading and Meditation: Matthew 28:16–20

*" '... And surely I am with you always, to the very
end of the age.' " (v. 20)*

I f God expects every Christian to be involved in the task
of making disciples, then we must stop thinking of
evangelism as an élitist activity – something undertaken
solely by ministers, priests and itinerant preachers.

Most Christians, whenever they hear the word "evangelist", think of someone like Billy Graham who goes from
place to place bringing people to a point of decision, and
then moving on. This kind of ministry is quite valid, of
course, for God has put certain people in the Church for
this purpose. You may not be called to this type of ministry,
but you are most certainly called to the ministry of making
disciples.

HOW DO WE MAKE DISCIPLES?

How do we make disciples? We do it by telling others the
story of Jesus Christ, by helping them come to a point of
decision, by encouraging them to become linked with a live
Christian church, and by demonstrating to them, by our
love and our actions, the reality of life in the kingdom
of God. If you are about to wilt under the enormity of the
task – take heart. Jesus Christ says, "Surely I am with you
always, to the very end of the age." Roland Allen says of this
statement, "The promised presence of Christ is not a reward
offered to those who obey, but rather the assurance that
those commanded *will* be able to obey." Get rid of the idea
that evangelism is something we do for Jesus Christ. It is
not. It is something He does through us. He does not say,
"Go out into the world and do something for Me." Rather
He says, "As you go into the world, to the office, to school,
to the factory, I am with you and in you making My authority known throughout the earth."

*You are
called to
the min-
istry of
making
disciples.*

Lord Jesus, I am relieved that evangelism is not just a commission but a co-mission. I may be ordinary, but with You I am
extra-ordinary. Together we can change the world! Amen.

PERSONAL EXPERIENCE

For Reading and Meditation: Hebrews 3:7–19

"… Today, if you hear his voice, do not harden your hearts …" (v. 15)

W e shall now move on and examine together some of the reasons why Christians do not share their faith.

If, as we have seen, the New Testament places so much emphasis on the need for personal evangelism, why are so many indifferent to this great demand? When one thinks of a convinced Communist or the hot enthusiasm of the soap box orators running around with their latest nostrums for curing the world's ills, how sad it is that so many church-goers are tepid concerning this vital task.

A LACK OF ZEAL

There are, of course, many explanations for this lack of zeal. Perhaps it's because of *a lack of a deep personal experience of God*. You attend church regularly, participate in all its functions, even teach in the Sunday School, yet you lack a personal relationship with God and His Son, Jesus Christ. You travel along on the strength of last Sunday's sermon or the last good inspirational service, but as far as a daily relationship with God, through prayer and Bible reading, is concerned, you know nothing of that. Consequently, having no personal relationship with God, you have nothing to give away.

If I am accurately describing your condition, then the first step you should take after finishing this page is to put down this book, kneel before God in prayer and invite Jesus Christ into your life as Saviour and Lord. Say, "Lord Jesus Christ, I am sorry that for so long I have tried to run my life on my terms. Now I invite You in. Forgive my sin and help me to live for You day by day." Believe me, if you will do this, it will not be long before your life becomes contagious and compelling.

If you have no personal relationship with God, you have nothing to give away.

Father God, I see so clearly that the effective proclamation of the Christian faith flows out of a personal encounter with You. Help me to experience this today. And if I have experienced it, then let its wonder deepen from this very moment. In Jesus' Name. Amen.

NOT ENOUGH BIBLE KNOWLEDGE

For Reading and Meditation: 2 Timothy 3:10–17

"All Scripture is God-breathed and is useful for teaching, rebuking, correcting and training in righteousness." (v. 16)

We continue discussing why so many of us fail to actively share our faith with the world.

A second reason why people fail to witness for Christ is *because they feel they do not have enough Bible knowledge.* If we wait to share Christ until we have a degree in theology or we have spent time researching answers to every conceivable question, then we will probably go through life without ever once testifying to our faith.

SPIRITUAL BABIES

Even spiritual "babies" can share what they have experienced. Remember the blind man who was healed by Jesus in John 9? Some critics tried to stump him with some pretty heavy theological questions, but he replied, "One thing I do know. I was blind but now I see!" (v. 25).

Beverley Shea, the well-known Christian singer, was asked by a friend, "How much do you know about God?" "Not very much," replied Bev, "but what I do know has changed my life."

This does not mean, of course, that we should be content with our ignorance. The fact that God can use us with a minimum of knowledge does not mean that we can ignore the Scriptural command to "Grow in the grace and knowledge of our Lord and Saviour Jesus Christ" (2 Peter 3:18).

THREE STEPS

I would suggest three steps for getting to know the Bible. (1) *Read it every day.* Apart from the readings in this devotional aid, go through the Bible systematically, book by book. (2) *Attend a weekly Bible study.* If you don't have an in-depth Bible study group in your church, then find one elsewhere and join it. (3) *Enrol in a Bible Correspondence Course.* To have someone supervise your pace and progress aids learning.

"What I do know about God has changed my life."

Heavenly Father, help me to strike a balance in this matter. To share my faith I need not wait until my Bible knowledge is perfect but, at the same time, I must "study to show myself a workman approved of God." Please help me. Amen.

"NOT A SALESMAN"
For Reading and Meditation: Exodus 4:1–17

"Moses said to the Lord, 'O Lord, I have never been eloquent ... I am slow of speech and tongue.' " (v. 10)

nother reason why people fail to share their faith is because, so they say, *they do not have the right temperament for talking to people.*

BROTHER LAWRENCE
A man said to me recently, "I do not have the personality for witnessing. I leave that to the 'salesman' types." Brother Lawrence tells how one day, sitting under a tree, he discovered a wonderful Christian secret. For some time he had been struggling to be an effective Christian but, as he looked at the tree, he thought to himself, "In the cool of winter the tree is barren and unfruitful. As spring comes new life comes and buds appear. Then in summer the fruit comes." He concluded that the tree was like his life, and there was no way he could make himself into a super personality for God to use. He could only trust God, in His own timing, to work through him and shape him into the person He wanted him to be. From that time onward, Brother Lawrence rested in what he called "the practice of the presence of God". Your weakest place can become your strongest place.

John R. Mott says that the phrase he has repeated most in his life is, "You can become strongest in your weakest place." Jeremiah, when the call of God came to him, pleaded, "I do not know how to speak; I am only a child" (Jeremiah 1:6). But he offered that trembling hesitation to God, and when he did speak, how mighty was his word. When God called Moses, he, too, pleaded that he was "slow of speech". But God met him at his weakest place, loosed him from his affliction and, when he got started, he made a speech that covered the whole book of Deuteronomy! He became strongest at his weakest place.

"You can become strongest in your weakest place."

O God, if this is so, then from today onward, I shall approach life with a new perspective. My weakness serves only to show up Your strength. In Your Name I say goodbye to my weakness and take instead Your omnipotence and strength. Amen.

TRUE TO ONESELF

For Reading and Meditation: Matthew 5:13–20

" 'You are the salt of the earth … You are the light of the world …' " (vv. 13–14)

A further reason why some Christians fail to witness is *because of the weight of their own personal problems.* "I have so many problems of my own," they say, "I would feel a hypocrite telling others that Christ can solve all their problems."

John White, a Christian psychiatrist in the USA, writes, "Has it never dawned upon you that the essence of witnessing is just plain honesty? You are salt – whether you feel like it or not. You are not told to act like salt, but to be what you are. You are a light. God has done a work in your life. Don't try to shine. Let that light God has put there shine out. Letting your light shine demands no more than honesty before unbelievers. In fact such honesty is, in itself, 90 per cent of witnessing. Witnessing is not putting on a 'Christian front' so as to convince prospective customers. Witnessing is being honest, that is, being true to what God has made you in your speech and in your day-to-day behaviour." Unbelievers know we are not perfect, and if we pretend we have no problems when we do, they will soon detect our dishonesty.

SUICIDE

I heard of a college girl who believed that in order to witness to her non-Christian roommate, she had to pretend that she had no problems whatsoever. Her roommate eventually became a Christian, but two weeks later committed suicide. She left a note saying she couldn't cope with her problems that she thought would have evaporated at her conversion. Let's be honest with the world. Coming to Christ does not mean that our problems disappear. It does mean, however, that we have Someone to steer us through our problems and turn them into possibilities.

"Honesty is, in itself, 90 per cent of witnessing."

O God, in my efforts to become an effective witness, help me not to put on a phoney front but to live out my life honestly, sincerely, and convincingly. This I ask in Jesus' Name. Amen.

FEAR OF REJECTION

For Reading and Meditation: Matthew 5:1–12

" 'Blessed are those who are persecuted because of righteousness, for theirs is the kingdom of heaven.' " (v. 10)

One of the biggest reasons why people fail to share their faith is *the fear of being rejected.*

MARTYR

And let's face it – rejection by others can be a very real possibility whenever we begin to witness for Christ. In fact, as someone has pointed out, this possibility is implied in the very word *witness.* The word *witness* in the Greek is *marturia,* which is the root of our word *martyr.* "An authentic witness," claims one preacher, "always carries the seed of the martyr." Jesus made it quite clear that if we are going to follow Him then we must expect some rejection. After all, was He not "despised and rejected by men" (Isaiah 53:3)? "He came to that which was his own, but his own did not receive him" (John 1:11).

One of the first things we should teach a new Christian is that, when they share their faith, they will sometimes experience a degree of rejection. This will not put them off – it will help deepen their commitment. They will then reason thus: "Am I committed enough to Jesus Christ to be willing to let people know that I am a Christian, even if it brings hostility from my relatives and friends?" Of course, whenever we face opposition or rejection, as a result of our witness, we will feel a degree of fear. The question we must then ask ourselves is this: "Who or what is going to rule my life – fear or Jesus Christ?"

"Who or what is going to rule my life – fear or Jesus Christ?"

AFRAID TO WITNESS

I once said to a woman, who told me she was afraid to witness, "I believe you are a coward." I waited for the explosion but it never came. Instead she said, "You are right. From now on it will not be cowardice but courage." "And courage," said someone, "is just fear that has said its prayers."

O God, You know the biting hesitation and doubt that fill my heart, when I feel rejected by those I love. But I hear You calling me to a deeper commitment. Help me to come out on Your side in this issue. In Jesus' Name. Amen.

No Obvious Response
For Reading and Meditation: 1 Corinthians 3:1–11

*"So neither he who plants nor he who waters is anything,
but only God, who makes things grow." (v. 7)*

We have been looking at some of the reasons why
Christians fail to share their faith, and today we come
to the last of these, which is *discouragement due to no obvious
results.*

Such a person says, "I have tried to witness but it doesn't
seem to accomplish anything. So what's the use?" This attitude stems from the fact that one feels inwardly compelled
to come up with results. *Evangelism is not defined by a posi-
tive response on the part of those to whom we witness.* God has
called us to do two things: (1) Proclaim the good news, and
(2) disciple those who respond for Christ. The actual producing of results is always in God's hands.

FAITHFULNESS
The text for today spells this out quite clearly. Look at it
again: "Neither he who plants nor he who waters is anything, but only God, who makes things grow." What God
expects from each of us is faithfulness, obedience and reli-
ability. "It is required that those who have been given a
trust must prove faithful" (1 Corinthians 4:2). If our efforts
do not yield results, it may be right, of course, to ask ourselves whether or not our approach is right, or whether our
evangelism is Biblical. If we are sure that we are doing
everything God expects of us then we leave the matter with
Him, and carry on witnessing whether we see results or not.

A LINK IN GOD'S CHAIN
Remember, too, that your witness may be an important link
in God's chain. I led a man to Christ some years ago who
told me that, ten years earlier, someone witnessed to him at
Hyde Park Corner and invited him to come to Christ. He
refused, but he confessed that he had been waiting for ten
years for someone else to ask him.

*The actual
producing
of results is
always in
God's
hands.*

**Gracious Father, thank You for reminding me that evangelism is
more than just a responsibility – it is my response to Your
ability. It is mine to speak, but Yours to save. I am so thankful.
Amen.**

AN ENLARGED HEART

For Reading and Meditation: 2 Corinthians 6:1–11

"We have spoken freely to you, Corinthians, and opened wide our hearts to you." (v. 11)

I suppose, if we are really honest, most of the reasons we have looked at as to why Christians fail to share their faith, are not really reasons – but excuses.

EVANGELISE MY HEART

If we were really gripped by God, then many of the issues we have discussed would dissolve as easily as the morning mist in the warmth of the rising sun. This is why I feel it is time now to bring the whole subject of evangelism into an intensely personal perspective by inviting you to ask yourself this question: *How much of a grip does God have upon me?* We are about to engage in some concentrated evangelistic effort, not to the hearts of the unconverted, but to our own hearts. The reason for this is because no one can be successful in evangelism until their own heart has first been evangelised by the Master. The poet put it thus:

> I know a bosom which within
> Contains the world's sad counterpart
> 'Tis here the reign of death and sin
> *O God, evangelise my heart!*

Evangelise my heart! What an exciting thought! Is not this exactly what we need? Assuredly it is, but in what way can God answer that prayer?

He does it by flowing into our beings with such an inrush of His life and power that our hearts actually become enlarged. Not physically, of course, but enlarged in sympathy, empathy and spiritual concern. Paul, as we see from our text, had a heart like that. Let me put it to you now. Is your heart like the apostle's – large enough to take in others? If not, then let God perform the operation that will bring about an enlargement of your heart.

Is your heart like the apostle's – large enough to take in others?

O God, Your Word is as sharp as a surgeon's knife, and just as saving. Open up my heart, I pray, and enlarge it until it is big enough to take in the whole wide world. In Jesus' Name. Amen.

For Reading and Meditation: Philippians 2:1–13

"Let Christ Jesus be your example ... For he, who had always been God by nature ... stripped himself of all privilege ..." (vv. 5–7, J. B. Phillips)

Today we begin with a pointed question: How does God go about the task of expanding a Christian's heart?

LOVE FOR ALL HUMANITY

Firstly, He does it *by giving us a great love for all humanity.* Many of us spend our lives in compartments. We move among people of our own social status. We talk most freely with those who are our equals, and, more often than not, we avoid the company of those whom we consider are beneath us in dignity, education and background. Love is the answer – a love that is deep, strong and true, and loves even when it cannot like. Christ is able to bring into our lives a stream of love for the lost that provides us with the power to go on loving even though we are rebuffed, rejected and reviled. It is almost impossible to love a drunkard who staggers along the road and finishes up in the gutter; our natural reaction is to turn away in disgust. But such is the love that Christ plants in our hearts, in response to prayer, that there is no situation we will ever face that cannot be answered by that love.

CHRIST'S SKILL

In the *Letters of James Smethan,* it is recorded: "Christ takes your view of things and mentions no other. He takes the old woman's view of things and shows a great interest in washing powder; Sir Isaac Newton's view of things and wings with him among the stars; the artist's view of things and feeds among the lilies; the lawyer's view of things and shares his sense of justice. But He never plays the lawyer or the philosopher or the artist to the old woman. *He is above that littleness."* The skill Christ has in relating to people, He passes on to us. It is ours for the asking.

A love that loves even when it cannot like.

O God, if this skill which comes from You is mine for the asking, then I ask for it today. Help me to use it to bring others to You. Amen.

SHEEP WITHOUT A SHEPHERD

For Reading and Meditation: Mark 6:30–44

"As he landed he saw a great throng, and he had compassion on them, because they were like sheep without a shepherd ..." (v. 34, RSV)

Another way in which Christ enlarges and expands our hearts is *by showing us what people really need.*

Bishop Taylor Smith, when responsible for the selection of chaplains for His Majesty's Forces, was once approached by a clergyman who asked to be considered for the job of chaplain. The bishop looked at him, pulled out his watch and said, "I am a soldier dying on the battlefield with three minutes to live – what have you to say to me?" Utterly taken aback, the man had nothing to say and, because he had no message for a dying man, his application was dismissed.

THREE MINUTES

If all of life was suddenly reduced to three minutes, it would be easy to see what people *most* needed. There would be hardly any doubt in a Christian's mind – *Christ!* Because life goes on and no one knows the exact moment eternity will call, it does not mean that people's needs are different. Christ is still the greatest need of all those who do not know Him and, as we draw close to Christ's heart, this single fact is brought fully into focus. When Peter and the rest of the disciples walked out of the upper room on the Day of Pentecost, they moved with tremendous urgency among the people. And why? Because they saw the people as Christ saw them – like sheep without a shepherd. When Christians get near to Christ's heart, they show the same emotion as the poet who wrote:

Christ is still the greatest need of all those who do not know Him.

Then with a rush the intolerable craving
Shivers through me like a trumpet call
O to save these! to perish for their saving
Die for their life, be offered for them all!

O God, as I ponder this fact, that the greatest need of my friends and family is Christ, let it burn within me until it catches fire. Then help me to share Christ with them – with love, enthusiasm and compassion. In Jesus' Name. Amen.

NO OTHER PLAN

For Reading and Meditation: Romans 10:12–21

"... how can they believe in the one of whom they have not heard? And how can they hear without someone preaching to them?" (v. 14)

We continue meditating on the ways by which God seeks to evangelise our hearts, thus expanding our vision and enlarging our concern for a world lost in sin.

Another way He does it is by reminding us that unless the good news is shared by those of us who have tasted it and experienced it, *there is no other way it can be made known*. God has no alternative plan! In his book *The Master Plan of Evangelism,* Robert E. Coleman shows how God's plan for the evangelisation of the world centres on what he calls "the redeemed winning the unredeemed". In other words, the only valid messengers of the Gospel are those who have themselves experienced its transforming power in their lives. Angels would vie with archangels for the privilege of telling the good news to the world but, having never tasted it, they cannot properly tell it.

A story I heard many years ago – whose source I have been unable to trace – tells how Christ, having ascended to His Father from the Mount of Olives, was immediately surrounded by a group of excited angels. Now that His mission was finished, they were eager to discover if they were to have any part in making the good news known. Christ explains to them that He has left this part of the task to His disciples. "But what if they fail?" asked one of the angels. "Didn't they prove untrustworthy in the past? Surely, Master, You can't leave the responsibility of making the message known solely to those disciples?"

Christ looked at the angel solemnly, and quietly said, "I have no other plan." Let this truth take hold of you now. If you and I don't spread the Word, then, quite simply, the task will not get done. God has no other plan.

If you and I don't spread the Word, the task will not get done.

O God my Father, with one stroke You bring everything out into the open and put it in perspective. In the light of Your Word to me today, I ask myself: What my heart has experienced, shall my tongue refuse to tell? Amen.

POWER FOR THE TASK

For Reading and Meditation: Acts 1:1–14

"But you will receive power when the Holy Spirit comes on you; and you will be my witnesses in Jerusalem ... Judea ... Samaria, and to the ends of the earth." (v. 8)

F inally, another way in which Christ evangelises and enlarges the hearts of His children is *by imparting to them a special supply of divine power.*

No one can expect to have a great deal of success in reaching people for Christ until they have been filled with the power that makes effective evangelism possible. This power is expressly promised by Christ to all His children and is, in fact, the biggest single factor in producing an enlarged heart.

NO LONGER AFRAID

Watch how it operated in the lives of the disciples. Before they received this power, they sat like frightened sheep in that upper room at Jerusalem "for fear of the Jews". Then suddenly there burst into the room the supernatural power of the Holy Spirit which, entering their personalities, transformed them from timid, hesitant disciples into men who were ablaze and invincible. No longer were they afraid of people's opinions. In fact, after Pentecost, they were the ones that largely shaped public opinion and, by their words and deeds, did much to change the trends of their day and generation. When you examine the lives of the disciples, prior to Pentecost, you cannot help but be struck by the fact that they had little interest in reaching the multitudes. They tried to keep Christ for themselves. On the Mount of Transfiguration, Peter seemed to be saying, "Let's build three tabernacles and stay right here." But all this is reversed at Pentecost.

The power they received enlarged their hearts, not only to take in Jerusalem, but also Judea and Samaria ... until ultimately they took in the whole of the then known world.

This power is expressly promised by Christ to all His children.

Gracious God, I see that, in giving me the gift of the Holy Spirit, You made it possible for me to meet the impossible. Help me to walk in the certainty that the task ahead of me is never as great as the power behind me. In Jesus' Name. Amen.

EQUIPPING THE LAITY

For Reading and Meditation: Ephesians 4:1–15

*"It was he who gave some ... to prepare God's
people for works of service ..." (vv. 11–12)*

I t is time now to give our minds to the question of what
part each local church plays in this vital and important
matter of evangelism.

IDENTITY CRISIS

In a day of rugged individualism and the plethora of what we
call para-church organisations, we must not forget that the
community of God's people, who form a local church, lies at
the centre of His purposes Regrettably, many local churches
– not all – are suffering from a severe case of identity crisis.

Dr Howard Hendricks says, "The contemporary Christian church is like an amnesia victim trying to find out
'Who am I?' " There are many reasons why the Church fails
to function in the way God desires, but I believe the major
one is this – God's people have not locked into God's Game
Plan which He has outlined in Ephesians 4:11–12. Imagine
for a moment you are standing on the sidelines at a football match. Suddenly, instead of the eleven men you expect
from your home team, just one man appears – the coach.
Someone says that as he has a lot more experience than the
others, he is going to play the other team all by himself.
Ridiculous? Well, isn't this the kind of picture many Christians have of the Church? The members expect the minister
to do all the preaching, praying and witnessing because, as
they say, "That's what he's paid for."

The Church will not move forward until everyone rec-
ognises that God gives leaders to the Church, not to do all
the work, but to help the rest of God's people do it. Lay
people are not in the Church simply to pay pastors, evangelists and teachers to do the Lord's work. Rather, pastors,
teachers and the other leadership are there to equip the so-
called "lay" people to be ministers.

*The "lay"
people must
become the
ministers.*

**O God, bring Your Church to the realisation of Your perfect
plan as outlined so clearly in Your Word. Use those in spiritual
authority over me as a tool in Your hand to make me more
useful and effective for You. In Jesus' Name. Amen.**

"WITHOUT LOVE – A CLANGING CYMBAL"
For Reading and Meditation: John 15:17–27

" 'This is my command:
Love each other.' " (v. 17)

We continue facing the strong challenge of Ephesians 4:11–12, which describes the Church as a community where the leaders equip the so-called laity for maximum effectiveness in Christ's Body.

I realise, of course, that some will now take what I am saying and start making comparisons with their own local church. If you find yourself in a church where there is no systematic training or teaching programme designed to help you discover and develop your basic spiritual gifts, do not go off the deep end and start taking pot shots at the minister or the church council.

PRAY
Firstly, pray about it. It may be that your minister has not quite caught the vision of this section of the Scriptures. Prayer can change things. Whatever you do, do not criticise, grumble or complain. This will only make you part of the problem and not part of the solution.

A SPIRIT OF LOVE
Constructive change can only come about in any church when it is done in a spirit of love. Remember, no evangelism, whether corporate or individual, is effective unless it is conducted in a spirit of genuine Christian love. "We Christians," says Dr Leighton Ford, "talk about 'winning the world to God.' We know the whole world will not be converted, but what if it were? What would a world won to Christ be like? Would its personal relationships be like those in your church? Would its educational system be patterned after your Sunday school? Would its political system operate like your church board?" If God's total Church is the agent for evangelism, then, remember, it can only be effective when it flows out of a spirit of love.

Evangelism can only be effective when it flows out of a spirit of love.

Lord Jesus, today You have touched the nerve centre of my problems. You know my tendency to criticise and complain. Give me a fresh glimpse of Your love – for to love more I must first see how much You love me. Amen.

THE KEY TO THE FUTURE
For Reading and Meditation: 2 Timothy 2:1–15

*"And the things you have heard me say ...
entrust to reliable men who will also be
qualified to teach others." (v. 2)*

W e ministers, priests, missionaries and evangelists are never by ourselves going to make a great impact upon the world. There are too few of us, and even if we could do it, it would be counter-productive, for it would take away from the laity that spiritual growth and development which comes through sharing one's faith.

THE PEOPLE OF GOD
At Pentecost the Holy Spirit was not given merely to the apostles, but to all 120 disciples. A Roman Catholic priest was asked, "What is the Church?" He replied, "The people of God." He was then asked, "Not the hierarchy?" His reply was the same, "No, the people of God." He was right. The word laity comes from the Greek *laos,* and means just that – the people of God. The whole purpose of what some people call "the hierarchy" is to equip God's people for the work of the ministry. Not merely for taking up collections, showing people to their seats and sitting on committees – which are necessary and important tasks, of course – but far more than that – training the people of God to be efficient and effective ministers. The chief business of leaders in Christ's Church is to be the guides, coaches and stimulators of a powerful lay movement, for lay witnessing is the key to the future.

Jesus was a layman. The religious system of His day gave Him no credentials. His call was from God and not from man. He was not ordained in the ordinary sense by the laying on of hands, His credentials were the changed people that surrounded Him. You, too, may have no credentials and no ordination, but, as a member of Christ's Body, you are part of His purposes in bringing the soiled and sinful to the Master's feet.

At Pentecost the Holy Spirit was given to all 120 disciples.

O Father, I am seeing so clearly that in Your Church everyone is expected to be a minister. Though some have more gifts and greater responsibilities, all are expected to serve. Minister to me so that I may minister to others. For Jesus' sake. Amen.

THE MASTER SOULWINNER

For Reading and Meditation: John 3:1–13

"… 'I tell you the truth, no-one can see the kingdom of God unless he is born again.'" (v. 3)

We come now to an important and practical section of our studies – *getting the message through.*

Over the next few days we shall endeavour to collect some of the important guiding principles we need to know when attempting to lead a person to new life in Christ. And where better to gather these principles than from watching the Master Soulwinner at work – Jesus Christ Himself. "Jesus," said a little boy, "is the Gospel in living colour." He is! Almost everything our Saviour did, while He was here on earth, was directed towards winning men and women to His Father's kingdom.

Someone has pointed out that every parable Christ spoke was a soulwinning parable. Although the four Gospels record only about fifty days in the life of our Lord, those days are filled with incidents, accounts and words that are directed toward helping people find hope and salvation in God. As we listen to His words, watch His acts and see His spiritual expertise, we build up a picture of One who strode through this life with one dominating passion filling His being – the passion of sharing the love of His Father with a soiled and sin-stained world.

Every parable Christ spoke was a soulwinning parable.

JOURNEYING AND TEACHING

On one occasion the Scriptures said of Him that, as He made His way to Jerusalem for the last time to face the cross, He came "journeying and teaching" (Luke 13:22, RSV). Many of us would have nursed our coming pain. But He had the inward compulsion to teach the love of God to others – on the way to die! If this Christ doesn't get into our blood and raise our spiritual temperature, then we ought to wonder why.

Lord Jesus Christ, I come to You to put my life alongside Yours, to be guided, directed and taught by You this day. Amen.

NO PROSELYTISM

For Reading and Meditation: John 4:1–4

"The Pharisees heard that Jesus was gaining and baptising more disciples than John ... When the Lord learned of this, he left Judea ..." (vv. 1 & 3)

We said yesterday that in order to find some guiding principles to help us win others to the new life in Christ, we are going to watch the Master at work.

THE WOMAN AT THE WELL

I know of no greater illustration of how to lead a person to faith and trust in God than the story of our Saviour's encounter with the woman at the well. So, just as an apprentice stands at the side of his master to watch and learn how a task is done, we come alongside our Lord in this gripping story and learn step by step as we go.

The first principle that becomes clear is that Christ was not interested in proselytising, but in bringing about a true change in human nature. The account says, "When the Lord learned that the Pharisees had heard of Jesus gaining and baptising more disciples than John ... he left Judea and went back to Galilee" (vv. 1 & 3, Moffatt). He would not allow Himself to become involved in a struggle for numbers – so He left at high tide. This account of the Samaritan woman is not in the context of proselytising, but of true conversion. Proselytising is influencing someone to change from one group to another without any necessary change in character and life. The Christian convert in the New Testament is never called a "proselyte" – there were Jewish proselytes, but no Christian proselytes. The Gospel produces not a change of label, but a change of life.

Those of us who may hesitate to throw ourselves into mass evangelism, because we don't want to become involved in just a scramble for numbers, are reassured here: this is deeper – it is a move to produce conversion.

The Gospel produces not a change of label, but a change of life.

O Father, help me to keep before me the fact that, in bringing someone to You, I am helping them not merely to change their label, but to change their life. In Jesus' Name I ask it. Amen.

USING THE INEVITABLE
For Reading and Meditation: John 4:4–8

"Now he had to go through Samaria." (v. 4)

We continue studying the thrilling account of our Saviour's meeting with the Samaritan woman. The Scripture says, "He had to pass through Samaria" (v. 4, RSV). As Jesus left Judea on His way to Galilee, He travelled through Samaria as it was the shortest and most direct route. Most Jews, because of their intense hatred and dislike for the Samaritans, would go by a more circuitous route along the Jordan valley, thus adding 60 or 70 extra miles to their journey. Jesus, however, banished such bigotry, took a straight course and thus found His evangelistic opportunity in something that was inevitable. Doing the right thing is always the right thing to do. Jesus found His opportunity of getting His message across in the everyday inevitabilities of life.

AS NATURAL AS BREATHING

There are certain things in your life and mine that are right and inevitable – we have to go to the office, to school, to the workshop, or perhaps attend to home duties. Evangelise that inevitable situation – find your opportunity in the inevitable contacts of the day. Evangelism is not something imported into special weeks, special days or special occasions – it must become as natural to us as breathing.

A businessman told me that he couldn't do evangelistic work as too many people came to him each day with their problems. I suggested to him that he might find his evangelistic opportunity right there – and he did. Once we have the will to evangelise, then it won't be long before God gives us the opportunity. Then no day is ordinary as all contacts become redemptive. Nothing – absolutely nothing – is more important under heaven than just that.

Once we have the will to evangelise, God gives us the opportunity.

Gracious heavenly Father, give me an alert heart and a responsive will so that I may discover an evangelistic opportunity in all my daily contacts. In Jesus' Name I ask it. Amen.

THE DOMINANT INTEREST
For Reading and Meditation: John 4:9–13

"Jesus answered, 'Everyone who drinks this water will be thirsty again ...'" (v. 13)

As the first step in opening a conversation is the most difficult, today we shall examine just how Jesus overcame this problem.

He began at the woman's dominant interest and led her along the line of that dominant interest. He began at the thing she came for – water – and then went from natural water to spiritual water. Is a young man interested in athletics? Then talk to him about a strong body and the necessity of purity if that body is to be at its best. It is part of the dynamic of the Gospel to enable a person to become pure not only in body but also in mind. Is a parent wrapped up in his or her children? Then it becomes a simple thing to show them how, if they want to pass on a good heritage to their children, they can best do it by accepting Christ and letting Him become involved in their family relationships.

One minister tells how, as a young evangelist, he stopped one night by a fence where the town drunk was working in his garden. The evangelist complimented the man on his fine garden, and then gradually brought the conversation around to the subject of whether he had got the weeds out of his own heart. This remark, made tenderly and appealingly, got right into his soul. He became a Christian.

GUINEA PIGS

The late Dr W. E. Sangster said that he knew a man in his sixties who took up keeping guinea pigs in order to reach a boy's heart. It might seem absurd and quixotic, but it proved effective. The boy, himself, became a fisher of men. When you show an interest in what people are interested in, they will probably respond and be interested in what you are interested in.

Show an interest in what people are interested in.

O Father, give me Your skill and insight to see what people want, and then to lead them from that want to what they ought to want. For Jesus' sake. Amen.

THE HIGHER ISSUE

For Reading and Meditation: John 4:9–15

" 'But whoever drinks the water I give him will never thirst ...' " (v. 14)

When Jesus found the dominant interest in the Samaritan woman's mind and opened up the conversation at that point, the woman reacted by putting up a barrier.

A SECOND INSTINCT

This is natural and instinctive – the instinct of self-preservation. Many Christians would have stopped right there, but they would have stopped too soon. If you hang around, a second instinct comes into operation – the instinct of self-revelation. If the first instinct is to shut people out, the second one is to open up. But to do this, a person has to feel that the one to whom they are talking is genuinely interested, truly sympathetic and warmly understanding. So don't be discouraged when you meet this instinct; wait for the working of that deeper instinct of self-revelation.

A PRINCIPLE

Now how did Jesus get rid of the clash between Jew and Samaritan which came into the picture at this point? " 'How is it that you, a Jew, ask a drink of me, a woman of Samaria?' " (v. 9, RSV). He did it by a simple technique which He used all the way through the conversation: He raised a higher issue – "living water". When He focused her attention on that higher issue, the smaller issue faded into the background and was forgotten. Fix that as a principle in an evangelistic conversation. Don't pick up subordinate issues and debate them; you will get tangled up in the little and the irrelevant. Raise the higher issue, and the lesser issue will fade out. This does not mean, of course, that you ignore a genuine objection. But as the issue you are raising – eternal life – is the greatest issue of all time, keep moving toward your goal, not theirs.

Keep moving toward your goal, not theirs.

O God, help me to be a guide who directs others toward Your goals. Help me to be too big to be caught up in little issues when larger ones await me. Amen.

THE DELICATE MOMENT
For Reading and Meditation: John 4:15–23

"The woman said to him, 'Sir, give me this water ...' " (v. 15)

J esus expressed an amazing confidence in this woman of Samaria: "If you knew the gift of God and who it is that asks you for a drink, you would have asked him ..." (v. 10). In other words, if you can see what I am talking about, you will want it. Jesus believes in people when they cannot believe in themselves. We must believe in people in spite of what they are if we are to influence them. If we become cynical about people we become powerless to help them.

A FURTHER CONTROVERSY

At this stage, the woman raised a further controversy: "Are you greater than our father Jacob?" (v. 12). Jesus could have said, "Jacob was a scheming liar and gained his birthright dishonestly." To have done so, however, would have started an argument. How did Jesus get rid of Jacob? Once again He raised a higher issue: "A spring of water welling up to eternal life." She got her eyes on that, and Jacob vanished out of the picture. It was then that Jesus came to the root cause of her difficulties – her moral problem.

Take it as an axiom in dealing with the unconverted that there is a moral problem in everyone's life. This is the decision point from which people move toward deeper darkness or toward the light. How did Jesus get to the moral problem without seeming to invade sanctities? He did it delicately. He did not say, "You are an adulteress", but "Go, call your husband." She then responded by saying, "I have no husband." The words mean more than they seem. It was an admission of guilt in itself. It is not enough to point out people's sins; they must be led to point them out themselves. Then, and only then, are they on the road to getting rid of them.

We must believe in people in spite of what they are if we are to influence them.

O God, my Father, help me to love love out of the loveless, and when I come to that delicate moment of sin exposure, give me the sure word that points to the sin exit – You. Amen.

THE GOAL

For Reading and Meditation: John 4:24–30

" 'Come, see a man who told me everything I ever did. Could this be the Christ?' " (v. 29)

We must spend one last day in looking at this marvellous encounter of Jesus with the woman of Samaria. We left the woman yesterday having come face to face with her sins. Feeling uncomfortable – as everyone does when they come face to face with their sin – she sought to divert the conversation on to an abstract religious issue: "Where should we worship?"

RED HERRING

Beware of the attempt to put you off the real thing by using the red herring of religious issues. Hold to the moral problem. Did Jesus answer her question? He did, but He was soon back at the central issue. We must not dodge questions or treat them as trivial, but keep the conversation moving toward the central issue – how a person can get rid of sin and find moral and spiritual deliverance. The moral problem is always central. We now ask ourselves: What was the end of this conversation, the goal toward which it all moved? It was this: "I who speak to you am he." The goal was the unveiling of Himself as Saviour and Lord. The end of our work in evangelism is to get people to see Jesus.

PRODUCING AN EVANGELIST

The end of our work in evangelism is to get people to see Jesus.

But there is one final step I want you to notice before we leave this matchless story. The woman left her water jar, went into the city and said, "Come, see a man who told me everything I ever did." The end of evangelism is to produce an evangelist. Someone said, "You haven't got them in until you get them out." The account says: "Many of the Samaritans from that town believed in him because of the woman's testimony" (v. 39). Jesus must have rejoiced that day that He had put the graft of a higher life into a human soul. That was the will of God for Him – it is also for us.

O God, help me to keep my life moving toward this central necessity and give me the ability to put the graft of Your life into other lives. For Jesus' sake I ask it. Amen.

An Evangelistic Lifestyle
For Reading and Meditation: 1 Peter 2:1–16

"Live such good lives among the pagans that, though they accuse you of doing wrong, they may see your good deeds and glorify God ..." (v. 12)

Our thoughts over the next few days will be centred on the need to develop an "evangelistic lifestyle".

We begin with a pointed question: Is our evangelism something we keep for Sundays and special occasions – or is it something that permeates all our actions and activities? Some Christians think of evangelism as something that fits into their lives like a section of a news magazine. There are headings such as sport, fashion, education, religion and so on, but nothing really ties or integrates these different sections except the staples and the cover. They feel that unless the activity in which they are engaged happens to fall under the section of religion, then it is inappropriate to mention their allegiance to the Lord Jesus Christ. Evangelism, for them, is seen as something done at a particular time and on special occasions. Although familiar with Jesus' statement, "You are the light of the world" (Matthew 5:14), they interpret this to mean, "when and where I want to be." Evangelism, however, if it is to be Biblical, must be a lifestyle.

Being true to God

Let me remind you once again of what the Christian psychiatrist, John White, has said: "Witnessing is not putting on a 'Christian front' so as to convince prospective customers. Witnessing is being honest, that is, being true to what God has made you in your speech and in your day-by-day behaviour." If we Christians are to be the salt of the earth, then we must get out of the salt shaker. Salt in the shaker never flavoured anything. And too much salt in one place tastes terrible and makes one sick!

Evangelism, if it is to be Biblical, must be a lifestyle.

Father, I see so clearly that the dominant impression I leave on people is my evangelism. Help me to make that dominant impression one that leaves people feeling that they have been in touch with an ambassador of Jesus Christ. Amen.

"STILL IN THE PENCIL"

For Reading and Meditation: Acts 5:33–42

"Day after day ... they never stopped teaching and proclaiming the good news that Jesus is the Christ." (v. 42)

We ended yesterday by saying that if we Christians are to be an influence in the world, then we must get out of the salt shaker and allow Christ's love to flow through us to everyone we meet. In other words, we must begin to develop an evangelistic lifestyle.

DEEP RELATIONSHIP

How do we begin? Do we start by determining in our minds that we will ask every non-Christian we come across point-blank, "Are you saved?" No. First, *we begin by making sure that we have a deep, rich, on-going relationship with Christ every day of our lives.* This point has been strongly emphasised in one of our earlier readings, but it will bear repeating here.

Professor Chad Walsh, in his book *Early Christians of the First Century,* said, "I suspect that Satan has called off his attempt to convert people to agnosticism. After all, if a man travels far enough away from Christianity, he is liable to see it in perspective and decide that it is true. It is much safer, from Satan's point of view, to vaccinate a man with a mild case of Christianity so as to protect him from the real disease." No one could accuse the Early Church of being "vaccinated with a mild case of Christianity." They had the "real disease" – and, believe me, they made it communicable.

A little girl was asked by her teacher where the dot was that should have gone over the 'i' in her composition. The little girl replied, "Oh, that's still in the pencil." Perhaps you have been withholding your witness far too long – it is still in you. Then get it out quick, for if you do not you will probably have little to witness to.

Perhaps you have been withholding your witness far too long.

O Father, make my tongue a dedicated tongue – dedicated to the highest possible use – that of witnessing for You. This I ask in Christ's Name. Amen.

GOD'S CONVERSATIONALIST

For Reading and Meditation: Psalm 107:1–15

*"Let the redeemed of the Lord
say so ..." (v. 2, RSV)*

We continue examining the steps we need to take if we are to develop an evangelistic lifestyle.

Second, *be alert to sharing Christ through your everyday conversation*. In an age when conversation is so superficial, it is simply amazing the number of people who are willing to talk deeply about spiritual things, providing they can do so with someone who speaks in a normal tone of voice and does not embarrass them with a style of language about which they know nothing.

A LONDON TRAMP

A preacher tells of overhearing a woman witness for Christ to a London tramp. Fragments of her speech floated to him thus: "It must be 'yea' and 'amen' to the promises of God ... I suspect you are still under the old dispensation ... Do you understand the difference between natural and effectual faith? ... You need to experience a mighty outpouring of the Spirit ..." The tramp's reply to all this was interesting. "Okey dokey," he said. The preacher said, "I felt two worlds had met in those two persons – and they had not intersected."

Be alert to sharing Christ through your everyday conversation.

Billy Graham, although a pulpit evangelist, is also a master of the art of bringing Christ into his everyday conversation. Leighton Ford, his brother-in-law, says of him, "We might be sitting at a table with some people and Billy will say, 'Last week I was talking with someone about this very same thing. I said ...' He then lets the rest listen in on a conversation he had with someone else. He gets the message home without people feeling he is preaching."

THE USE OF QUESTIONS

Remember the use of questions in opening up conversation. "What do you think is wrong with the world?" "What's your goal in life?" Let's begin today to grasp the opportunities that come for being a conversationalist for God.

O God, give me, I pray, the skill that puts You right at the centre of my conversation and in a way that impresses, not embarrasses, those with whom I speak. In Jesus' Name. Amen.

THE USE OF LITERATURE

For Reading and Meditation: Psalm 126:1–6

"He who goes out weeping, carrying seed to sow, will return with songs of joy, carrying sheaves with him." (v. 6)

The third step in developing an evangelistic lifestyle is that of *sharing Christ through carefully selected literature.* Multitudes of men and women will be in heaven through reading a book that was given to them by someone deeply concerned about their salvation.

I once said to a university lecturer who, whenever we met, seemed to always want to argue with me about the Resurrection, "Here's a book I'd like you to read; when you get through, I'd be interested in knowing your impressions." He read it and was immediately converted. He told me later, "I was really wanting to hear my own voice and my skill at sustaining an argument. The book you gave me allowed me no real opportunity to do that, so I just sat back and let Christ save me."

SELECT A BOOK

In one of the CWR Institutes in Christian Counselling, a lady said that she spent £1–£2 a week on evangelistic literature for her non-Christian friends. Her technique was this: she waited until she discovered someone's dominant interest – politics, education, science, etc. – then selected a book written by a Christian that presented Christ in the context of that subject. She told us that she aimed to do this for about thirty to forty of her non-Christian friends each year. Someone asked her what results she got from this. She said that she knew for a certainty that around ten people each year were brought to Christ through this simple but effective ministry.

Discover the dominant interest of a non-Christian friend, and then pass on a book written from a Christian perspective on that subject. It may be the means in God's hands of winning them to Christ.

Share Christ through carefully selected literature.

O God, give me a creative mind and imagination in order to help me win my friends to You. Guide me to the right seed, for I intend to be a sower, sowing beside all waters. For Your own Name's sake. Amen.

"For His Sake"

For Reading and Meditation: Colossians 3:16–25

"And whatever you do, whether in word or deed, do it all in the name of the Lord Jesus ..." (v. 17)

Another step we can take in developing an evangelistic lifestyle is *to share Christ through our daily work.* Unfortunately, many Christians never realise that their work is a major area of Christian stewardship.

Attitude to work

Sloppiness and slipshod attitudes toward our work will result in ridicule and scorn whenever we attempt to openly share the Gospel. "The Christian workman," says one writer, "is not an ordinary workman, extraordinary only because he goes to church and not to the cinema on a Sunday evening. He is a different *workman.* The Christian employer is not an ordinary employer who happens to give large sums to the Church. He is a different *employer."* In humble and exalted positions, we Christians must see life from the standpoint of Almighty God and seek to share Him in every situation.

Are you a doctor? Then every time you take someone's temperature, do it with the tenderness and compassion of Christ. Are you a nurse? Then show God's love to everyone on your ward – including that cantankerous person in the end bed! Are you a schoolteacher? Then show by your demeanour before your class that you are not only an educator, but an ambassador for the Lord Jesus Christ. Are you an office worker? Then show by the way you tot up the columns or type a letter that you are working not merely for an earthly employer, but for the King of kings.

A lecturer in a teachers' training college was asked by one of his pupils what was different about him from the others. "Perhaps," he said, "it's because every lecture I give I know there sits in my audience the Lord Jesus Christ."

A Christian's work is a major area of Christian stewardship.

O Father, my destiny is so clear. I am to live for You and not for myself. Help me to represent You before everyone I meet and in everything I do today. For Jesus' sake. Amen.

"A Ready Listener"

For Reading and Meditation: James 1:16–27

"Understand [this], my beloved brethren. Let every man be quick to hear, (a ready listener) ..."
(v. 19, Amplified Bible)

Another way we can go about developing an evangelistic lifestyle is by *learning how to be a good listener.*

This aspect of sharing our faith has been greatly neglected. Instead of listening sensitively to what a person is saying, we wait for an opportunity to proclaim the truth. And the result? The truth we try to communicate fails to penetrate deeply into other people's lives. Someone has described this as the "Evangelical disease": it's the habit so many of us have fallen into of giving answers before we have properly listened to the question.

DIALOGUE OF THE DEAF

Dr Paul Tournier, the famous Swiss psychologist, says, "It is impossible to overemphasise the immense need human beings have to be listened to ... in most conversations, although there is a good deal of talking, there is no *real* listening; such conversations are no more than a dialogue of the deaf."

It's not easy to be a good listener. Most of us, when talking to someone, want to offer advice or tell them as quickly as we can that they need Christ. Although it may be hard for some to understand, the more time we give to listening to someone, the easier it is for them to respond when we share with them the true solution to all their problems – Christ. The Bible says in Proverbs 15:23, "Everyone enjoys giving good advice ..." but adds, in verse 28 of the same chapter, "A good man thinks before he speaks" (TLB). Remember, sharing your faith does not always mean *talking.* Perhaps, as someone said, this is why God gave us two ears and only one mouth: He might want us to do twice as much listening as talking.

God might want us to do twice as much listening as talking.

Heavenly Father, make me a real listener, one who can rub a spiritual finger along the edge of a person's soul and discern his real needs. Make me sensitive and not obtrusive. For Jesus' sake. Amen.

A DEDICATED TONGUE

For Reading and Meditation: Psalm 45:1–8

"My heart is stirred by a noble theme as I recite my verses for the king; my tongue is the pen of a skilful writer." (v. 1)

We have been seeking to answer the question: Is our evangelism to be confined to certain periods and special occasions or is it to be a constant lifestyle?

NON-VERBAL

I believe the answer is inescapable. Christ wants us to carry our witness with us everywhere we go and to everyone we meet. This does not mean, of course, that we have to but-tonhole everyone we meet and ask them, "Are you saved?" But it does mean that by using every non-verbal means we can, we share with them the fact that Christ lives in us and that we are the adopted children of a heavenly King.

To do this effectively means that we have to develop a certain amount of creativity in our relationships with those who are non-Christians. God has gifted us with a great deal of creativity, and where better to use it than in thinking up ways of how we can make Christ meaningful to the people we meet. We said yesterday that listening is important, but there are times when listening is not enough. We must *tell* people about Christ – clearly and convincingly. Let me put it this way.

Suppose you had a fatal disease from which happily you were delivered through the efforts of a certain doctor. One day you meet someone with exactly the same symptoms as you once had. Would you simply listen and say, "Oh, I'm so sorry. You have my deepest sympathy?" To do so would be almost criminal. No, instead you would say, "I had the very same disease – would you like to know how I was cured?" When people meet us they get a dominant impression – an impression of self-centredness or an impression of Christ-centredness. What sort of impression are people getting from you?

Are people getting an impression of self-centredness or of Christ-centredness?

Lord, help me to be more than a half-witness, someone who acts and does not speak or someone who speaks and does not act. I want to be a whole witness and witness with my total life. Amen.

A Picture of Evangelism

For Reading and Meditation: Jude verses 17–25

"Snatch others from the fire and save them; to others show mercy, mixed with fear – hating even the clothing stained by corrupted flesh." (v. 23)

Much of what we have been saying up until now has been confined to the theory of evangelism. It is time now to turn to more practical things.

"Philosophers," wrote Karl Marx, "have only interpreted the world differently; the point is, however, to *change* it." We can never expect to change the world by focusing merely on the theory of evangelism; what we have learned must now be put to work.

An artist

An artist once set out to capture on canvas the meaning of evangelism. He painted a picture of a storm at sea. Black clouds filled the sky and, illuminated by a flash of lightning, a little boat was being dashed against a reef by the pounding seas. In the water sailors could be seen struggling for their lives. The only glimmer of hope was in the foreground. There a huge rock jutted out of the sea, and clinging desperately to it with both hands was a lone seaman. It was a moving scene but after the artist stepped back to admire his work, he sensed that he had missed the point.

So putting aside the painting, he immediately started work on another. It was the same scene, the same black clouds, the same flash of lightning, the same ship and the same lone seaman clinging to a rock. But the artist made one change. This time the lone seaman was holding on to the rock with just one hand, and with the other was reaching down beneath the waves to lift up a sinking friend. That is the New Testament picture of evangelism – with one hand we hold on to Christ, and with the other we reach down beneath the swirling waters of sin to help lift up a friend.

With one hand we hold on to Christ, and with the other we reach down to help lift up a friend.

Father, I'm available. Use me to lift someone from the seas of sin. Take over my whole being and turn me from theory to practice. In Jesus' Name. Amen.

PRAYER AND EVANGELISM
For Reading and Meditation: Mark 11:12–26

" 'Therefore I tell you, whatever you ask for in prayer, believe that you have received it, and it will be yours.' " (v. 24)

I n seeking to turn theory into practice, we shall now consider some of the practical steps we can take in attempting to win our acquaintances, friends and relatives to the Lord Jesus Christ.

"The best way to begin to witness," said someone, "is to begin to witness." For those who are not actively engaged in evangelism, let me lay down some guidelines to help you get started. Remember, however, that these are guidelines and not rules. It may be, as you think them through and pray over them, that God will show you something different.

Prayerfully draw up a list of people who you know are not Christians and begin to pray daily for their conversion.

FIVE FRIENDS

George Müller of Bristol, the famous man of faith and prayer, once did this. He prayerfully selected five friends whom he wanted to see become Christians, and began to pray for them every day. Within about five years, two of them came to Christ. Twenty years later, one more came. He kept on praying for the other two day after day for forty years until he died. Both of the two remaining men on his prayer list became Christians within two years after his death!

If the people you select live close to you, then you can consider inviting them to a Christian event such as an evangelistic rally or concert. You might like also to consider giving them a Christian book, or plan a day out with them on some friendship activity, where you share with them something about your Christian faith.

What is most important is to begin right away. Ask God to show you those for whom He wants you to pray – then go to work in daily intercession for their salvation.

Pray daily for their conversion.

Thank You, Father, for reminding me again of the power of prevailing prayer. As one great servant of Yours once said, I shall "ask great things from God, expect great things from God, attempt great things for God." Help me, I pray. Amen.

Your Own Personal Story
For Reading and Meditation: Acts 26:1–20

" 'King Agrippa, I consider myself fortunate to stand before you today as I make my defence ...' " (v. 2)

We continue looking at practical ways by which we can win our friends, acquaintances and relatives to faith in the Lord Jesus Christ.

Today we consider the importance of learning to tell our own personal story.

Not only did the early Christians tell the story of Jesus but they told their own story. Paul did this with great effect on at least two occasions (Acts 22 & 26). The early Christians did not, of course, advance their experience as the main reason why others should believe. Our experience is not the basis of our faith – it is the validation of our faith. Sharing Jesus consists first of telling His story and then our own story. People who are unconvinced by the theoretical are often moved by the personal.

A close observer of Billy Graham says that whenever he is struggling to put some point across, he stops preaching and begins to relate how, as a young boy of seventeen, he came to know Jesus Christ. The observer writes, "Almost always a hush seems to fall over the audience." Each one of us has a story that is worth sharing because every person is different and, from the heart of your uniqueness, God wants to bring forth a testimony to His Son. Every Christian should think through his own conversion story and tell it clearly, effectively and concisely in about 90 seconds.

FOUR THINGS

A testimony to Christ should underline four things: (1) Your attitudes to life before you came to know Christ. (2) How you came to feel your need of Him. (3) How you came to know Him. (4) What has happened since – what Jesus Christ means in your life at this present moment.

Sharing Jesus consists first of telling His story and then our own story.

Lord, I am so grateful for my own uniqueness. No one else in the universe has a story quite like mine. Help me to tell it convincingly and compellingly. For Your own dear Name's sake. Amen.

STRESS REPENTANCE
For Reading and Meditation: Mark 1:14–20

"... Jesus went into Galilee, proclaiming ... 'The kingdom of God is near. Repent and believe the good news!' " (vv. 14–15)

Some Christians, although they are able to relate their own personal story of how they found Christ, find it difficult to summarise their faith in a Scriptural setting. You do not need to know the whole Bible in order to lead a person to Jesus Christ, but there are some basic things which need to be firmly embedded in your memory.

These basics are illustrated for us in the passage before us today, and show us clearly the three things that one needs to know in order to become a Christian. The first is repentance. "Repent and believe the good news." Do not be afraid of this word when talking to your non-Christian friends for evangelism, to be effective, must tell "the truth, the whole truth and nothing but the truth". Repentance means "agreeing with God." When I repent, I recognise that God made me for Himself, for Him to live and reign in the centre of my being, and that I have no right to manage my life on my own terms. Many people think repentance involves great emotion. It can do, of course, but primarily it is an attitude of mind whereby I stop trying to manage my own life and allow Jesus Christ to be my rightful Lord.

A U-TURN

Don't sugar-coat or try to soft-sell this issue.

Don't sugar-coat or try to soft-sell this issue. People who come into the Church without experiencing true repentance are full of problems. Explain to them that repentance is like driving down life's road in your car when suddenly Christ confronts you. You realise you are going the wrong way, so you move over and let Him come in, take the steering wheel and make a U-turn. Then you start heading in a new and different direction.

O God, impress deep into my spirit today the profound importance of this truth that to become an effective Christian, one must enter through the door of true repentance. Help me to make this clear to everyone to whom I witness. In Jesus' Name. Amen.

FOCUS ON JESUS CHRIST

For Reading and Meditation: Mark 1:14–18

"... Jesus went into Galilee, proclaiming the good news of God ... 'The kingdom of God is near ... believe the good news!' " (vv. 14–15)

We continue examining the basic requirements which a person must fulfil in order to receive Christ and become a true Christian. The first thing, as we saw, is repentance.

What, then, is step 2? This: "Believe the Gospel." The Gospel is basically the good news that God has done in Jesus Christ what we could never do for ourselves. To believe is to put our full trust and confidence in the message of God's Word. How do we convey this? We need to stress three very important points, all focusing on the uniqueness of our Lord Jesus Christ.

HE IS GOD'S SON

(1) *He is unique because He is God's one and only Son* (John 3:16, 5:18 and 10:30). This makes Him not only the Son of God but God, the Son. In a day when there are so many self-appointed saviours, gurus and so-called prophets, take time to impress upon the person to whom you are talking the fact that Jesus Christ alone is *the* Son of God, and not *a* son of God.

HE TOOK OUR PLACE

(2) *He is unique because only He could take our place on Calvary and pay the penalty for our sin* (Matthew 26:28, 1 Corinthians 15:2–4). Christ actually became man for our sakes so that He could take our place on Calvary's tree, substituting His righteousness for our guilt so that He might bring us back to God (1 Peter 3:18).

HE ROSE FROM THE DEAD

(3) *He is unique because He rose from the dead* (Luke 24:36–48). No sceptic has been able to explain how the first Christians, who were so defeated when Jesus died, suddenly became triumphant witnesses. The change can only be explained by the fact that He rose from the dead to live His life within the personalities of His disciples.

To believe is to put our full trust and confidence in the message of God's Word.

O Father, help me to get this clearly in my mind so that I, in turn, can make it clear to others. Impress it upon me so that, when I share it with others, I will be able to impress it upon them. Amen.

ENCOURAGE PERSONAL COMMITMENT
For Reading and Meditation: Mark 1:16–20

" 'Come follow me,' Jesus said, 'and I will make you fishers of men.' " (v. 17)

The third basic essential which is needed in presenting a clear picture of salvation to someone who does not know Christ is this – *"Follow Me."* Conversion means more than just an intellectual assent to what Jesus said and did; it is a personal relationship with Him in the here and now.

Someone put it this way: "In becoming a Christian there is not only something to believe, but also Someone to receive." Some like to compare it to marriage. Marriage is more than a philosophy or an institution. I may spend years studying the social implications of marriage, but unless I have a partner to whom I am personally related, marriage remains merely a theory and not a fact. A person may well study Christianity for years and yet have no personal relationship with Jesus Christ. This fact, then, must be stressed – Christianity is not just an adherence to a formula or a creed, but a vital contact with a living Person.

"SPIRITUAL MIDWIVES"

One of the most delightful experiences life can offer us is to be on hand when God breaks creatively into someone's life in true conversion. It's like observing the birth of a child! We need to think of ourselves as "spiritual midwives" and watch for those whom God is drawing to Himself so that we may aid them. In helping a person come to Christ, we ought to avoid manipulating them or playing on their emotions. Don't try to persuade people in a way that restricts their freedom. We must urge people lovingly, persuade them with all the conviction of our being – but we must watch for God's moment and be sure not to push people until they are ready.

"There is not only something to believe, but also Someone to receive."

O Father, make me sensitive to the fact that fruit cannot be picked until it is ripe. Give me insight and understanding so that my efforts coincide with Yours, and do not contradict them. In Jesus' Name. Amen.

GETTING THE DECISION

For Reading and Meditation: Romans 10:1–13

"As the Scripture says, 'Anyone who trusts in him will never be put to shame.' " (v. 11)

What if, after witnessing to someone about the Gospel and the need for faith in the Lord Jesus Christ, they say, "I would like to become a Christian – can you help me?"

SCARED

The first person I witnessed to, about a month after my conversion, did just that: he said, "I would like to become a Christian; how do I go about it?" I was scared out of my wits. I began to physically tremble and stutter but somehow, as we say, I "got him in". Let me encourage you to step out in faith and let God use you. There is no joy in this world that exceeds the joy of leading someone to the Lord Jesus Christ. There are several ways this can be done.

Firstly, you can suggest the person gets alone somewhere, tell them the kind of prayer they should pray and then invite them to tell you about it afterwards. *Secondly,* you can introduce your friend to someone else who can pray with them and lead them to Christ – but this ought to be done only if you feel utterly inadequate and unable to deal with the situation.

Thirdly, and this is without doubt the most rewarding way, get the person to pray with you. If the person shows some hesitancy in praying then you can lead them in a prayer – pausing and letting them repeat the words themselves. It is best if this prayer is prayed aloud, because the ear then comes to the aid of the mind and helps to clinch the decision in an important way. Then, when this is over, ask the person a pointed question such as this: "What has happened to you today?" This will gently press them to make their first confession – "I have taken Jesus Christ to be my personal Saviour."

> *Step out in faith and let God use you.*

O God, make me ready so that soon I can personally become involved in experiencing one of the greatest joys a Christian can know – the joy of leading someone to new life in You. For Jesus' sake I pray. Amen.

THE IMPULSE TO SHARE

For Reading and Meditation: Acts 6:1–8

"... choose seven men ... full of the Spirit and wisdom. We will turn this responsibility over to them. They chose ... Philip ..." (vv. 3–5)

The conclusion which we have reached, then, after six weeks of study, is this – evangelism is not something imposed on the Church; it is something inherent. The work of winning men and women to Jesus Christ is not merely an occupation but an outcome – it is the outcome of the nature of life itself. Inherent in all life is the impulse to create – life produces life. If it doesn't create it dies.

PHILIP THE EVANGELIST

The impulse to share life is wonderfully illustrated in the life of Philip. He was given a task by the Early Church which was not intended to be evangelistic. In fact, the apostles gave up the work of serving tables so that they could give more of their time to evangelism. But, strangely enough, the only man who had the title of "Evangelist" in the Acts of the Apostles was the man who had a layman's task imposed upon him and who was not supposed to get involved in evangelistic work. The impulse to share Christ, however, was greater than the imposition. The reach of his soul went beyond the reach of his hand and, although delegated to share out the goods and serve tables, he became involved also in sharing the Gospel and became known affectionately in the Scriptures as "Philip the evangelist" (Acts 21:8). In fact, this lay evangelist became so active that he kept the apostles on the trot following up his ministry. "When the apostles in Jerusalem heard that Samaria had accepted the word of God, they sent Peter and John to them" (Acts 8:14).

I say again, evangelism is not something imposed; it is inherent. We cancel the power of the Gospel in ourselves unless we pass on its power to others.

Evangelism is not something imposed; it is inherent.

O God, if the expression of my faith is the essence of my faith then help me to so live that my faith becomes contagious, convincing and compelling. In Jesus' Name. Amen.

NO PRIVATE WORLD

For Reading and Meditation: I Peter 3:8–22

"... Always be prepared to give an answer to everyone who asks you to give the reason for the hope that you have ..." (v. 15)

We are emphasising the urgency and importance of evangelism.

There are three cardinal signs indicative of the new life in Christ: (1) the desire to pray and read the Scriptures; (2) the urge to join others in Christian fellowship; and (3) the desire to bring others to Jesus Christ. Some have even gone as far as to say that without the last-named, there is no new life. Bishop Stephen Neill once said, "It is not for any minister to say, 'I am not an evangelist'. The minister has been ordained for the purpose of winning men and women to Jesus Christ, and if he is not doing it then it should be questioned whether he ought to be in the ministry at all. So with a layman; if he is not willing to be a witness, it is time he gave up calling himself a Christian."

NO EVANGELISM: NO CHURCH!

Strong words, but they are words that need to be said. And why? Because if the Church fails to win others to Christ then, quite simply, there will be no Church in the future. This is not the main motive for evangelism, of course, but it is a fact that cannot be overlooked. When we of the Church of today die, the Church dies with us – unless the Church of tomorrow has been won in the meantime. If you, as a member, fail to win anyone else, you have a part in the death of the Church. If others fail with you, then there will be no Christian Church one hundred years from now. Any Christian who thinks he can live in a private world of his own is an idiot. That is what the word "idiot" literally means – one who lives in a private world. There are no private worlds. We belong to each other – for good or ill.

Pray and read the Scriptures; join others in Christian fellowship; bring others to Jesus Christ.

O God, give me the will to evangelise my daily contacts, for I know if I have the will then it won't be long before I have the opportunity. In Jesus' Name. Amen.

CHRISTIAN CONTAGION
For Reading and Meditation: Philippians 1:1–21

"... being confident of this, that he who began a good work in you will carry it on to completion until the day of Christ Jesus." (v. 6)

The urgency and importance of evangelism which we are discussing does not arise simply from the call of Christian leaders but from the very words of Christ Himself: "Go into all the world and preach the good news to all creation" (Mark 16:15). Evangelism is not an imposition – something imposed on us by zealous ministers and priests, but an exposition – something exposed out of the very facts of Christian experience. Paul puts it this way: "You have contributed to the gospel from the very first day down to this moment; of this I am confident, that he who has begun the good work in you will go on completing it until the day of Jesus Christ" (Philippians 1:5–6, Moffatt). From the very first day they stepped into the kingdom of God, they began to contribute to it – to spread it. It was not something they learned; it was instinctive. It was as natural as a baby's cry at birth.

THE EXPRESSION OF FAITH

While we are thankful for the Christian leaders who called us to a "Decade of Evangelism" in the 1990s, the work of evangelism must not be seen as an imposition into a particular period of history; it is part and parcel of our Christian faith. Evangelism is ongoing. Why? Because once we begin to share our faith then our faith begins to mean something more to us. Christianity, you see, is not merely a conception – it is a contagion. And when the contagion is lost, the conception, too, is lost. It is a law of the mind that that which is not expressed soon dies. Nothing is really ours until we share it. The expression of our faith is of the essence of our faith.

Christianity is not merely a conception – it is a contagion.

O God, You have given me the greatest work in the world, the work of bringing others to You. Help me not only to dedicate myself to that task but to be faithful to it. For Jesus' sake. Amen.

A Seven-step Ladder
For Reading and Meditation: Psalm 51:10–19

"Restore to me the joy of your salvation ... Then I will teach transgressors your ways, and sinners will turn back to you." (vv. 12–13)

During the last few days of these readings on *Sharing Your Faith,* I want to spend some time recapitulating on what we have said, and looking once again at some of the more salient issues so that they will not be overlooked or forgotten.

A CONTAGIOUS LIFE

As we said yesterday, Christianity is contagious. Over the next three days we shall build what we are going to call *a ladder to a contagious life.* To have the qualities of Christ in our being is not enough unless we have also the quality of contagion. For contagion makes these qualities outgoing and places them at the disposal of others. Remember that "no heart is pure that is not passionate, no virtue is safe that is not enthusiastic", and no life is truly Christian that is not Christianising. We must deliberately set ourselves to be spiritually creative. If we climb the following seven steps, they will, I believe, help us towards a contagious life.

(1) *We are made in the inner structure of our beings to be creative.* You and I are made to achieve, to be outgoing, to create. If we are not positively creating and producing, the machinery of life will get out of gear, for we are geared to creation.

(2) *To win others to the new life is the highest form of creative activity.* In widening the circle of faith, so that it includes more and more people who have trusted Christ as their Saviour, we have a chance to be creative where it counts most. Although physical creativity may be denied us, spiritual creativity is an ever-open door. No Christian is denied spiritual creativity unless, of course, they deny it to themselves.

> *No life is truly Christian that is not Christianising.*

O God, I bring my non-creative life to You today so that You can touch it into creativity. Flow into my imagination so that I will be alert and open to ways by which I can win others to You. In Jesus' Name. Amen.

THROWING OFF ALL RESERVE

For Reading and Meditation: Acts 3:1–11

"Then Peter said, 'Silver or gold I do not have, but what I have I give you ...' " (v. 6)

We continue climbing the ladder to a contagious life.

SHARE IT WITH OTHERS

(3) *Nothing is really ours until we share it with others.* All expression deepens impression. It is a law of the mind that that which is not expressed dies. If there is no outflow, the inflow automatically stops. There are two seas in Palestine. One is the fresh and fruitful Galilee, the other, the Dead Sea – bitter and barren. Why the difference? Galilee both takes and gives – the Dead Sea has no outlet.

The passage before us today reminds us that "to have" is not enough. "What I have," said Peter, "I give!" My possessions become my debt. I do not *own* them; I *owe* them. I must share them.

THE WILL TO EVANGELISE

(4) *We shall have the will to evangelise.* Up until now the desire to evangelise has been mostly in our minds and our emotions; now it must get into our wills. We must decide to share with others what others have shared with us. We are at a place in our spiritual lives today similar to that of the early disciples in Acts 13:44–52. The apostles had gone to the Jews alone acting as if the Gospel was Jewish – from Jews to Jews. The Scripture says, *"Then, throwing off all reserve,* Paul and Barnabas said, 'We were bound to proclaim God's Message to you first. But since you spurn it ... we turn to the Gentiles' " (v. 46, Weymouth). The early disciples had a larger Gospel in their hearts than they were proclaiming. Today a similar crisis has arisen. We have a larger Gospel in our hearts than we are proclaiming. We have acted on less than the whole. Now the challenge of these readings is pressing us to throw off all reserve. Then our evangelism will be contagious, continuous and compelling.

Our evangelism will be contagious, continuous and compelling.

Gracious God and Heavenly Father, help me, from this very moment, to throw off all reserve and to act on the larger implications of the Gospel that I know are in my heart. For Jesus' sake. Amen.

"THE GENTLE INNER PUSH"

For Reading and Meditation: Romans 2:1–16

"... they show that the requirements of the law are written on their hearts, their consciences also bearing witness ..." (v. 15)

Today we come to the three final steps of our ladder.

A SECRET ALLY

(5) *If we are afraid of being snubbed or rejected we will remind ourselves that we have a secret ally in every heart.*

Victor Frankl, the famous psychiatrist, says that the God urge is native to man, as native as the other urges. If you suppress God in your life, he says, you will get a complex, just as you do when you suppress other urges. He believes that about 50 per cent of his patients are suffering from the suppression of the God urge in their lives. If that is true, it means that we have an ally in every human heart when we approach it and claim it for Christ. Deep down in every man and woman is that something which waits for somebody to give the gentle inner push that will lead them to Jesus Christ. All that keeps some people away from Christ is that they have never been asked.

FOR JESUS' SAKE

(6) *Our motive in winning people to Christ will not be to exploit our need for achievement, but we will do it for Jesus' sake.* A nurse stood washing the sores of a leper on the mission field. A visitor from the West stood watching her and remarked, "I wouldn't do that for a million pounds."

"Neither would I," said the nurse. "But I will do it for Jesus' sake." When we look into the face of Jesus and then into the face of humanity's need, we realise more fully the need to spend the balance of our days trying to bring them together.

(7) *If we fail we shall fail in doing what we should do.* But perhaps the greatest failure is the failure to do anything. If our efforts falter, perhaps it will give God the greater chance to work. When we speak haltingly it may be that He will speak most clearly.

Perhaps the greatest failure is the failure to do anything.

O God, help me, as I go through life, to be used by You in giving that gentle inner push to someone which will bring them to Your feet. For this is where the world belongs – at Your feet. I am there now. Please use me, dear Lord. Amen.

THE DIVINE EQUATION

For Reading and Meditation: John 20:19–31

"... 'As the Father has sent me, even so I send you.'" (v. 21, RSV)

On this last day of our series of readings on the tremendously important subject of *Sharing Your Faith,* we must sum up what we have been saying in a single conclusion.

THROUGH ME

And our conclusion is this. It is not enough to tell people that Jesus is the answer. We must be willing to say, "Jesus – *be* the answer through me." Is not this what our text is saying to us today? "As the Father has sent me ... so I send you." The words are in the form of a divine equation: As ... so. As God wrapped His love in the personality of Jesus Christ, so He wants to wrap His love in us today. He could have put His message for mankind in fiery flashes of lightning and scattered them across the sky. He could have organised a troop of singing angels to have gone from one end of the world to the other so that all mankind could hear. Instead He compressed Himself into the body of a man, walked the hot, dusty roads of Palestine and endured the agony of a cross so that mankind could not only hear but see the measure of His love.

He still chooses to spread His message through a human personality.

Today, as in those distant centuries close on 2,000 years ago, He still chooses to spread His message through a human personality. He chooses to walk the streets of Britain, the United States of America, indeed of every country in the world through interpreters of His Gospel such as you and me. I trust that soon everyone who has shared in these daily meditations will have the privilege of saying to another person, "I would like to introduce you to Jesus Christ", and of seeing that transforming friendship begin.

O God, I have looked into Your heart of love during these readings, and I can never be satisfied until I can get others to look into Your heart. I commit myself, in these coming days, to getting others committed to You. Help me to succeed. For Jesus' sake. Amen.

BE A GROWING CHRISTIAN
EVERY DAY

Every Day with Jesus for Growing Christians are born out of CWR's regular two month devotional Bible notes.

If you have found this special edition helpful, why not start reading **Every Day with Jesus** regularly? Join over half a million other readers worldwide benefitting from the daily . . .

ENCOURAGEMENT

INSPIRATION

CHALLENGE

THAT EVERY DAY WITH JESUS PROVIDES

Available from Christian bookshops, church agents or on subscription from CWR

SHARING YOUR FAITH

God expects everyone to play their part in fulfilling the Great Commission, but so many of us really struggle with evangelism. Selwyn Hughes provides us with practical guidelines to help us overcome our difficulties and shyness in sharing our faith.

- **Realise the urgency and importance of evangelism**
- **Practical guidelines for effective evangelism**
- **Learn confidence in sharing your faith with others**

EVERY DAY WITH JESUS FOR GROWING CHRISTIANS SERIES

Deepen your understanding of key areas of Christian living with this inspiring new series designed to increase personal maturity and effectiveness.

- **Seven weeks' material: start any time**
- **Daily approach enables the subject to be absorbed more easily**
- **Provides practical help and insight**
- **Leaders' guide available for home group use**

OTHER TITLES IN THE GROWING CHRISTIANS SERIES

Praise and Worship   Prayer   Relationships   Discipleship   Armour of God   Group Leaders' Guide

ISBN 1-85345-069-3

9 781853 450693